In Gravity Nation

*

for Zerra

yrs for art!

Chip Rawlins

2004

Western Literature Series

## Books by C. L. Rawlins

*A Ceremony on Bare Ground,* 1985

*Sky's Witness: A Year in the Wind River Range,* 1993

*Broken Country: Mountains & Memory,* 1996

*In Gravity National Park: Poems,* 1998

P     O     E     M     S

# In Gravity National Park

## C. L. Rawlins

*University of Nevada Press* ▲▲ *Reno & Las Vegas*

Western Literature Series

University of Nevada Press, Reno, Nevada 89557 USA

Copyright © 1984, 1987, 1988, 1989, 1991, 1994, 1995,

1996, 1997, 1998 by C. L. Rawlins

Manufactured in the United States of America

Design by Carrie Nelson House

Library of Congress Cataloging-in-Publication Data

Rawlins, C. L. (Clem L.)

In Gravity National Park : poems / C.L. Rawlins.

p.   cm. — (Western literature series)

ISBN 0-87417-322-1 (paperback : alk. paper)

1. Nature—Poetry. I. Title. II. Series.

PS3568.A849315   1998          98–22256

811'.54—dc21               CIP

The paper used in this book meets the requirements

of American National Standard for Information

Sciences—Permanence of Paper for Printed Library

Materials, ANSI Z39.48-1984. Binding materials were

selected for strength and durability.

First Printing

07 06 05 04 03 02 01 00 99 98

5 4 3 2 1

*To Kenneth Brewer, for his poetry, teaching, and friendship.*

# Contents

❹ For the Listener

# Acknowledgments

I'm grateful to independent presses and bookstores for their support of poetry, and to Stanford University for the Wallace Stegner Fellowship, to the Utah Wilderness Association for their Poetry Prize, and to the Poets & Writers Exchange Program and the Poetry Society of America for sponsorship of a reading tour. Further thanks go to the Wyoming Arts Council for the Blanchan Memorial Prize and the Wyoming Literature Fellowship.

Heartfelt thanks to Alden Borders, Katharine Coles, William Johnson, Carolyn Kizer, Denise Levertov, Trudy McMurrin, Sherman Paul, Linda Baker Rawlins, Richard Robbins, Timothy Schaffner, and Arthur Sze, who read the manuscript and helped in various ways.

Thanks also to Liz Arthur, G. Barnes, Steven Bauer, Moya Cannon, Peter Blue Cloud/Aroniawenrate, B. J. Buckley, Scott Cairns, Karen Chamberlain, Fidelito Cortes, John Daniel, Kenneth Fields, Art Goodtimes, Jeffrey Harrison, Gary Holthaus, Thomas Lux, Patricia McConnel, Neltje, Richard Poole, Chris Rawlins, and Frazier Russell, who responded to these poems with insight. If poetry in America is at times a lonely art, then you have made it much less so.

: : :

Thanks to the editors and staffs of the journals in which these poems first appeared: "Living in at least two worlds" and "An American Chinese" in *Boar's Tusk* (Spring 1984); "In Rock Springs, there will be a reading" in *Camas* (Spring 1998); "For Carmen Quintana" in *cold drill* (1991); "Old cars and trucks" in *Ellipsis* (1987); "Independence Day," 1988 in *Ellipsis* (1988); "I'll give night a body" in *Ellipsis* (1989); "The Hag" in *Ellipsis* (Spring 1995); "Elegy for Edward Abbey" in *High Country News* (10 April 1989); "Grace" and "The Rebound" in *Owen Wister Review* (Spring 1988); "Fires" in *Oxford Magazine 5*, no. 2 (1989); "Eleison" in *Petroglyph* 1, no. 1 (Spring 1989); "Paths, Crossing" in *Ploughshares* 20, no. 4 (Winter 1994–95);

"In Gravity National Park" in *Poetry Ireland Review* 44 (Spring 1995); "'Enter my dreams, love'," "For the Listener," and "Sacrament with pitcher pump" in *Poetry Ireland Review* 48 (Winter 1995–96); "Full October" and "Aspens" in *Poetry Wales* 30, no. 2 (September 1994); "The Mink" in *Poetry Wales* 31, no. 1 (July 1995); "Solvay Trona Mine, June 30, 1994" in *Poetry Wales* 31, no. 4 (April 1996); "Hypolimnion" in *Quarterly West* no. 41 (Autumn/Winter 1995–96); "Drinking in the Space" and "Elegy *for Edward Abbey*" in *Sequoia* 33, no. 1 (1989); "The Weight of Speech" (titled "Words") in *Shandoka* (1988); "The River" in *Utah Wilderness Association Newsletter* (1989); "All Souls Day" in *Weber Studies* 6, no. 1 (1989); "The River" in *Wild Duck Review* 3, no. 3 (August 1997); "The River" and "Old cars and trucks" in *Wilderness* (Summer 1989); "Late Friday, in December" (titled "The Bar") in *Wyoming, Hub of the Wheel* no. 7 (1990). "The River" has also been anthologized in *A Great and Peculiar Beauty*, ed. Thomas J. Lyon and Terry Tempest Williams (Layton, UT: Peregrine Smith, 1996), and *Wild Song: Poems of the Natural World*, ed. John Daniel (Athens: University of Georgia Press, 1998).

Epigraph credits: Page 1, Emily Dickinson (1233), reprinted by permission of the publishers and the Trustees of Amherst College from *The Poems of Emily Dickinson*, ed. Thomas H. Johnson (Cambridge, MA: The Belknap Press of Harvard University Press, Copyright © 1951, 1955, 1979, 1983 by the President and Fellows of Harvard College). Page 10, Pablo Neruda is quoted from a recording heard on National Public Radio, ca. 1983. Page 25, John Berger, "Romaine Lorquet," *About Looking* (New York: Vintage, 1991). Page 49, Wallace Stevens, "Peter Quince at the Clavier," *Collected Poems of Wallace Stevens* (New York: Alfred A. Knopf, 1923).

**1**

# A Sketch Map

*Had I not seen the Sun*

*I could have borne the shade*

*But Light a newer Wilderness*

*My Wilderness has made —*

*—Emily Dickinson*

# Eleison

You could go mad in these pines.
Trappist lodgepoles, crowded,
shift, and only moan or sigh.
Stand, standing, never waiting,
not in judgment nor in resignation,
with their dead all barked and bleached and mulching,
heaped like wheatstraw coarse about their feet.

And the wind breathes hard,
shovel-cold, uncomforting,
with no familiar reeks and memories,
hollow boxcars down the snowfield
in a flood of nothing. Clouds tear back,
above, cathedrals, granite wings and spires,
walls in which are cracks, no doors,
which only lead you up, across, along,
to lose you in the sky. Holy water
bleeding from the glacier, murky,
runneling through scree and shattered gravel
swells and freezes every clot of moss.
Wet boots, summits drowned
in roaring cloud. *In excelsis Deo.*
Cold enough to kill up here.

Huddled in this broken field, *Kyrie,*
the crevice seeming warm, though only still,
under talus big as houses buried in the wind;
the goddamn years it takes to lift a mountain;
in these bodies, mine and yours,
how precious little heat.

MOUNT BONNEVILLE, WYOMING

# Drifting in Montana

*for Carolyn K., after a poem by Tu Fu*

Dry grass and heaven's breath upon the banks,
waves chuckling on the hollow hulls, tied fast.

Stars spring up from ridges, black above
thirty miles of lake, one reflected moon.

Can love rise from the word alone?
A poet wakes to spoken dreams,

Apart. Dogs bark and drunken laughter
drowns the owl's dark flute.

FLATHEAD LAKE, MONTANA

# An American Chinese

Lacking traditional robes,
the moon is savage, gnaws
a white wound in a black lake.

In the wind-buffeted grove
a stampede of shadows:
lodgepole for bamboo.

If Li Po lived out here
he'd chug eight straight shots in the Cowboy,
bash his Blazer into a bull moose,
choke on a last *Godammit*, die
at ninety miles per hour.

BIG SANDY OPENING, WYOMING

The Chinese poet Li Po lived A.D. 701–62. There is a story—perhaps true—
that he drowned while drunk, leaning from a boat to embrace the reflec-
tion of the moon.

# The Rebound

*after a poem by Lin Ho-ching
though not much like it.*

Dirt road into trail,
I walk and dust settles
through scratchy old pines.

Between stumps, spider silks
part across my bare skin,
each distinct as a kiss.

Noplace to nowhere;
blue flax and yarrow,
a familiar ache.

Black pines to snow,
glacier to sky.
For now, content,

a damnfool grin.
Green moss and gold lichen
on boulders at rest.

Now I'll live without fear—
my friends, this fine rock,
this shadow right here.

WIND RIVER MOUNTAINS

# Living in at least two worlds

Back from the spring in the green draw
with water, galvanized pail half-full
bells against the doorframe, slops
(limestone water's sweet, granite water pure).
Stove rumbles, holding fire; the spilled drops
roll like a busted string of pearls on hot black iron.
Out back, four horses genuflect and sniff
the tight-latched oatbox lid. Life.

Radio sings with a woman's voice,
the song ends, I flip a cake,
watching the first sunbeam strike
a map of mountains, head south
down the line shack wall.

Fifty miles to the Boulder Store
on a road you hate after the first trip.
Regular as church: eggs, coffee, cheese,
apples, flour, rice, beans. Cartons
in the pickup bed, wedged with care.
Beer with Grant or Doc or Norm:
whoever got bucked off or too wet to bale.

I read letters in the truck, ask
but no one comes: work, school, new loves,
Alaska, France, New Zealand,
anyplace but here. I buy more beer.

Eleven thousand bumps and I'll be home,
left, left, right and the road ends up
at a boulderpile the glacier dropped.
I pop the gate loop, drive through, stop.

The horses dust up and wheel,
nip and buck and fart,
glad the Oat-Man's home.

BIG SANDY OPENING, WYOMING

# The Weight of Speech

Oh, but words are heavy,
they tumble out of us and fall
to laminate like bright, wet leaves.
Or stack like derelict cars, or scatter, broken glass,
a million tiny glints from railroad dirt,
which in gray heaven might be stars.

The condor carries poems she cannot lift.
Words tap the eggs of peregrine, which break,
and ballast the crops of teal with lead.
Dancing alone and blind in the world
they crush animal nations to dirt
and blacken skies with wasted oil.

Condensing from cool, collegial air
they distend the patient ear like wires
hung with bowling balls. Oak shelves groan
and fat tweed pockets fray as the word monsoon
sluices from the red-tiled roofs; the plaza fills,
the halls, the classrooms, offices, until
you climb the tower, thrust your head
inside the bell to be light and dry and free.

In time you'll find yourself
mute as light cascading on the rock.
Out here, looking down on the dialogue of roads
or up at silver sentences that stitch the blue.
Where gold October freezes on your lips,
rattles her leaves, empties out your book,
*goodbye, goodbye my love, goodbye,*
where nothing listens, and the real work begins.

BIG SANDY OPENING, WYOMING

# For Carmen Quintana

*You can cut the flowers,*
    *but you can't hold back the Spring.*
—*Pablo Neruda*

That night, it snowed.
The whole town lay content,
leafless, resting from the day.
I wished
for a yawning cat to stroke,
turned and clicked the radio,
you spoke:

   *They were like bulls,*
   *they were snorting like bulls*
   *as they set me on fire.*

# Fault and Thrust

*Formations are arranged in the legend*

*according to geographic extent, stratigraphy, and age.*

*Yet all these relationships are inherently inexact*

*and sometimes problematic.*

*—Geologic Highway Map of Wyoming, 1986*

# All Souls Day

*for Sharon*

The click of balls on the pool table
stitches me to my stool.
Five miners jostle, let the spring door slam
and sit down in their coats.

"If it starts," she says, and laughs,
"run in the john, sit down
and hold the door shut with your feet."

The ugly one is voiced
like iron tracks on sandstone,
rasps and booms to the bar
how he whipped his first wife's ass
for drinking beer with cowboys.
Cracks his gapped grin over her hands,
soft and brown, uncapping his first beer.

She smiles, like a canyon at a conqueror,
tenders his drink,
reserves herself.

He glares at me. I find fascination
in my beer: how bubbles form and rise,
burst and disappear.

The silence roars and rushes.
Under her old white sweater her breasts
are full and distant as clouds,
and her hung purse swings as she brushes past,
handwoven, brown and tan, rough wool
with a pattern of blue doves.

FERRON, UTAH

# In Rock Springs, there will be a reading

on the equinox. I take the poems that I'll return
to a writer just divorced, whose mother died
last year. She broods on youth and disillusionment.

The first hour, north of Eden, the desert folds like memory,
holding remnant snow on sheltered slopes; all else is dry.
The road's black curve is long and slow, the sky recedes,

blue ebb along the horizontal coast.
On the peaks, the snowline's high for March. Recollection
says late April, even May: an augury of smoke,

forests rising up in flame, and losses counted high.
My tires trace the asphalt line between small towns
with smaller reason to be here, maps of wish and lie.

The road's fenced—for every mile, three hundred posts,
four braces and one gate. Barbed wire glistens and the ravens
scatter as my shadow flies above their carrion smear—

a red blot with a jutting leg, a rabbit's ear. Cretaceous sand,
and yellow shale and gray, the Mesozoic beds of coal that hump
high to the east, the Rock Springs Uplift, pierced with mines,

shrugs the highway down its belly-seam. Of soda ash,
methane, oil, uranium, the troubled harvest of all things,
this urge, my going where I will, an envelope

of poems upon the seat. Divorce, democracy, and doubt.
Land where my father died. Of thee, and not alone, I sing.

BOULDER / FARSON / EDEN / ROCK SPRINGS

## Drinking in the Space

I come here for faces,
voices, glances, bodies full of blood.

All day aspens emptied out the sky,
gold tatters spinning down till only twigs
were left to finger the impending blue.

Clouds breathed one word: snow.
You could clamp the taste of storm
between your molars, wind

kicked willow leaves, bruise-brown,
across the sand to nest in shadow
under sage, a pillow for the cold.

The house, a vacuum, darker
than the space between two stars, atmosphere
too thin to hold an echo or a wife

says: you don't live here
and you never did, and I know nothing
of your history, your life.

Twelve miles to church
and two miles to the bar, I worship
close to home, a being

I can touch, a god who
goes to work each day,
a goddess, bourbon on her breath

who has strong wrists from bucking hay,
who raises sparks from worn-out denim, nips your earlobe,
draws you from the close and smoky temple,

from the brief embrace of light, urgently
out through the boot-scarred door
under the hovering storm, into the night.

BOULDER, WYOMING

# Grace

*for Leonard*

The kids endure him
better now than he, himself.
He won't disclose how old
he's grown in pain, what each breath costs,
the shame; can't tell his secret
any more than a leg-broke horse
could tell him.

He's seen it a thousand times: the gelding
butchered in the barbs, head bowed
to the bloody grass; the cow far gone,
heaving at a dead breech calf;
blue heeler kicked by a broody mare,
dragging dead legs.

What doctoring won't save, you spare
indignity: coyotes circle in, the ravens
peck still-seeing eyes. Can't make it good,
that awful patience, when a bullet
is the only gift. Death looks
to him as he must have looked
to any animal in pain: sudden,
looming black against the light.

He's read a book or two, named his rifle
Misery Cord and hefted its cold weight,
flinched at the blast, at his image fixed
in the mirrors of those eyes,
the shock and then the cloudy calm —
how many times? Seen
that last, quivering breath fly off,

and silence beckoning
beyond the deed.

BOULDER, WYOMING

## Winter in Parallel

Under night's breath,
where the avalanche runs out,
a space cleared by disaster,
we cross a field in snow.

Flanked by spruce and fir
where shadows gather,
shoulders touching, like the wives
of miners trapped by the explosion
gathered around the smoldering pit
for the nameless to be named.

In hidden profusion,
asters, lupines, larkspurs,
yellow rue, all frozen hard, bleed
color into snow, a kindness,
so, to die in bloom. So.

Each woman waited,
heard, wept. As the foreman turned away
they sang "The Rock of Ages" — God, why *that?*
His eyes were raw with sulfur smoke,
on the coarse wool of his cuff,
the snot froze hard.

So. Cold-breathed intention
rolls like a wave through all the rooms.
And the meadow spins, a constellation,
red and bronze and sapphire blue.

As they sing. As the foreman's boots
punch through the coal-starred crust.

And every slow departing step
gleams back, a brilliant white.

PRICE, UTAH

# Late Friday, in December

Sometimes, this is all we have —
strong drink, the bump of bodies in the smoke,
voices sounding twice off varnished pine;

When snow drifts as deep as losses in the lee
of every house, and short days glare, and go,
and each night pounds the membranes of these walls
with gusts and silences.

Felicity is tall, hard-eyed, her hair
coarse, cannon-barrel black. "Love's a debt,"
she says. Tin cup to catch heart's blood.

I watch the close and broken country of her eyes.
"You'll only want me once," she says,
and kills her drink and lifts her shoulders
to accept the weight of absences.

"I'm saving that," she says, and sighs —
"What's left?"

And so we dance
in the room of honey-colored light,
making of our soft collision one whole body,
all we know and want and cannot keep.
Then, without a word, I let her go.

She leaves, and cold comes in
before the door's shut tight. Nothing else
I need in this damned place tonight.
I go out to the windy dark.

It's snowing in her space.
The arc lamps bite on painted steel—
these cars in which we all go separate to our separate homes.
The snow flies quick and golden through the light,
and scatters, driven someplace on the wind.

BOULDER, WYOMING

# Aspens

*for Carolyn and John*

One chosen year in four,
leaves burn brighter at the equinox,
flame reflected in a lake at night.
None can say which year
the color's crux will come, but now
under frost, another burning crowns the fall;
one deep night could set the rain to snow.

Alone through aspen up from Willow Creek,
where two grouse waited on each other
by a boulder: she, composed and chuckling;
he, puffed and handsome, wings out
like open hands, throat distended,
tail erect, a year's desire drumming
through the hollow hill.

Grouse mate in the spring, I thought, and yet
I saw them there. Love's no stranger
than a pair of lovers to enhance the grove,
the ache of bodies woven. Leaves
were falling as they danced,
I smelled a snowstorm in the wind
and questioned nothing, watched,
and left them to the world.

Winter comes unargued
as the dark, to all. Love, amen.
Even in the fall of empires, even now
the aspens smolder, lovers marry,
and desire booms and struts
the darkening woods before the snow.

BIG FLAT-TOP MOUNTAIN

# I'll give night a body

She reclines on blue hills,
winter, her blanket.
Her arms covet mountains
asleep, her cold children.

I'll give her
long hair like a river of silence,
black on bare shoulders, full and unbound,
a forest to hide in, wing-folded darkness,
shadow her going, her love, her garment.

I'll give night a voice
like dry snow through black needles,
kiss of the ice, so hard and so hungry,
death to high rocks, cliffband and summit,
so stand our thoughts
and so she devours them,

and each broken bit
a life, a dream.

GROS VENTRE SLIDE, WYOMING

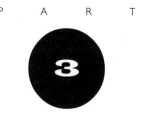

# The Closing of the Sky

*All art, which is based on a close observation of nature,*

*eventually changes the way nature is seen. Either it confirms*

*more strongly an already established way of seeing nature or*

*it proposes a new way. Until recently a whole cultural process*

*was involved; the artist observed nature: his work had a*

*place in the culture of his time and that culture mediated*

*between man and nature. In post-industrial societies this*

*no longer happens. The culture runs parallel to nature and*

*is completely insulated from it. Anything which enters*

*that culture has to sever its connections with nature.*

*—John Berger, "Romaine Lorquet," 1974*

# Paths, Crossing

*for Gary Holthaus*

Seven geese, southwest,
and seven flat-black ships, converging
in the Colorado sky, before

the pale haze of early winter,
bright and bronze and empty,
on a Sunday just approaching noon.

I count the birds again: seven.
And the helicopters: seven, in a line
northeast, their rotors blurred

and sounding faint percussion, high
above the freeway hum. Seven of each kind,
too perfect, almost every way, for trust,

the numbers, parallels and vectors,
sheer coincidence: the ancient memory of the geese,
a wargame on the seventh day.

The two flights cross and pass, I count again.
Exact. Their flight paths make a great ghost X, flat
and horizontal, signaling *unknown*.

And, true, I know near nothing of the geese
except they are alive, and nothing of the ships
except they carry unknown men,

uniformed and practicing
for a presumed event, a hard black presence
fuming in burnt air above the towns,

the teeming highway, muddy farms,
and ponds where geese still winter, in a world
where men have taken on black shells
and learned to fly.

NEAR LONGMONT, COLORADO

# Independence Day, 1988

It started that night—
kids and matches, fireworks, dry grass.
The Forest Service and the Pinedale Volunteers
sprayed water and went home to bed.

But next day, wind puffed up the smoky spots to flame
to running walls that chased the fire crews like a red-foot bull,
whooshing hill by hill along the Skyline Road,
and Pete Steele in the surplus pumper
drove into the smoke, was licked
by fire on the face.

Third degree, the *Round-Up* said,
and critical; they flew him to Salt Lake.
*Who were the kids?* asked someone in the bar,
but no one knew. Fifteen hundred acres
whipped to soot and stone. *Two years,*
said someone, *this will all be grass.*

The argument flared up again,
to pass a law against the sale and use. The lawyer said
it's not fair to the businessman who's paid good money
for his stock, fireworks, that is, bottle rockets,
sparklers, burning snakes,
and tiny bombs.

And that same day, the missile ship *Vincennes*
shot a plane of travelers to shreds above the Persian Gulf;
an aircraft, three hundred souls—a firework:
independence marked.

*Who were the kids?* asked someone
in the bar. *No matter,* someone answered,
*sage and bitterbrush — that thick stuff*
*aches to burn.*

PINEDALE, WYOMING

# The Master of Small Engines

The heart's a cylinder and piston,
so you'd think. He starts the blower,
revs, assaults a snowbank in the dark.
And Linda wakes with *dirty bastard*
rapping like an echo from her lips. Flat
hammers of exhaust tap every pane of glass

and resurrect the bitter neighborhood.
He boosts new-fallen snow from resting place
to sintered stack, cuts paths across his lawn
for neighbors who don't come or call,
carves one out back, where he used to sneak
a smoke, before—hard, the doctor's word.
Now, snow is more than snow. He cuts, blows,
piles, hews the flanks of every silent mound.

By March, one final drift, north in shadow,
lies along the house. He lets it melt,
heaves the mower from its winter den
for sympathetic magic, muttered oaths,
balm for wornout bearings, shims to squeeze
a wobble out. *The way things fall apart*
—sharpening the thin and scalloped shears—
*an old mechanic can't retire unless he wants to pay*
*some other S.O.B. It may not start.*

It does. He nods but doesn't smile; he'll never say
what sings for him, what for the rest of us is noise.
The blades are sharp. This early, nothing's green but faith.
Or loathing for the grass that wakes and wakes again

to raise a million spears. The steel heart will break.
*Wears out like every goddamn thing.* He'll curse

and coax a spark, love the racket and the long sap-bleeding swath,
should either of us live to see the spring.

LOGAN, UTAH

# Between Wars: Spring 1992

Dry grass and moisture in the ground,
a light wind in the west. The slow flame wanders
up the garden's flank, darkening the hopeful red
of wildrose suckers to burgundy or brown.

We herd the fire with old flat shovels, whack
the helpful demon down and steer it on. It wants
to gnaw on richer food, cornstalks purged and heaped,
prunings from the cottonwoods, the lumber stack.

It dodges in the heavy thatch, climbs the air,
and swirls round a cornerpost, as we pound
its quick, bright fingers into ash. As we tread
the barbed frontier

where old temptation burns, to let it loose.
We've mastered it so long, and know its use,
and know that, swift and strong, like truth
it dances in the barn and throws the old house

sparkling to the sky. I see the heat
behind her eyes, windows in a burning church,
long hair smoking golden out beneath her cap.
Another winter's passed us by without an end
to cold. Her neck's a lily root, pale device,

her people refugees, and mine, invasion
spreading like white virus in the blood. We burn
into the pasture, heading the march of flame
along the wind, beating at the narrow tongues
that want to merge and mount, exulting,

tangle in the rabbitbrush and flurry up the road,
to leave us breathless, barren in their sooty wake,
and, wingless, raise a black wing in the air.

BOULDER, WYOMING

# Fires

She comes in, on the whine of tires;
the oak door closes as she bends to kiss;
hair slips from her shoulder like suspended rain,
exhaust fumes holding to her skin like light.
No life or thing untouched;
behind a screen of ferns the brittle window
sings, the rain begins, sirens rise.

: : :

In Varanasi, in Bhopal,
a widow knows the stink of pyres,
beloved dead, the day's dead
a signature of ash upon the world. She grieves,
inhales black particles adrift; consuming fire to flesh
as rain to burnt ground — cuts and heals
and mixes ash in the river bed,
a thin, black stroke, the world's
one common tongue.

: : :

Fly, black babies, fly
skinny as insects, light as dust, whirl up:
the starving are no use, even to themselves, and you
look like the future, make our sandwiches taste
strange. Here, take this money, here,
black babies, now take heart,
take wing if you want,
but fly away.

: : :

Everything I touch burns my hand, look
this chrome car-door handle, this bridge toll coin,
look, the pause button on the stereo, the lightswitch, keys,

this devil-box, ski-bindings, credit cards, look, everything
I own has fire inside, ozone wreaths and sparks, this
woman's a catherine wheel, her breasts
white-pepper moons,
these words—
weapons.

: : :

On the north slope, 13th Avenue
balconies the glowing grid, City of the Saints.
Up here my friends dig in, nested deep in books and violins,
soft-footed, sweet dissenting mice in rented rooms.
Clear night, says G. We can see the valley
to the mountain's point; so volcanoes
watch their magma flow, the heavy,
molten beauty's right. For each
spur of light in this profusion
burn how many lives?

: : :

While gentle, well-intentioned
witnesses in wonder and despair look on,
just home from poetry and drinks, and call their come-ins
or goodnights, the holy city like a reliquary gleams,
radiates, consumes itself, crying
through our crowded dreams.
Fire. Fire. Fire.

SALT LAKE CITY, UTAH

# Tableau

The Landcruiser, ugly yellow, bashed,
rests upon its roof,
the black bull on his side.

The highway, a hard line between,
defines the fraction,
steel into flesh,
that won't reduce.

The windows of the car
give back the hills;
the bull's black eyes,
now smudged with death,

were glossy pools of sense.
When night's head swung,
so heavy, to the headlong rush,

grew eyes that burned the headlamps back,
did the driver manage half a word?

Dawn. The pale grass is still.
Frost grows and glistens white
on rusty muffler, tires, frame,

the black bulk of the bull —
diamonds in a hard, new light.

FONTENELLE, WYOMING

# Hypolimnion

The big fish lie down deep, feathering
the rim of rock that drops off into dark
and holds the heavy water, waiting to be ice again.
The hungry slash and burn, no wiser than the rich,
wars raise their smoky hymns. Burnt air
accumulates, a new religion,
dying as it grows.

The distant peaks
we counted, ten years gone,
are myths, existing for the map and not the eye.
This air's like grey wool glued to skin. The lake,
remote as heaven in a glaciated cup, thaws
before its time: no legends drive

the thermocline, but simple heat —
Old Sun, whose bets collect.

The surface water lies in strata
like clear stone, assorted by its heat.
I glide above the deep, where density abides.
Where schools of cutthroat spark the leafy light,
holding under the heat, in the hypolimnion,
like refugees — crowded, crying
on the black frontier.

BLACK JOE LAKE, WYOMING

# On Knife Point Glacier

In your heart I burned, faulty bearing
fused to muddy fire, defective part. Escaped
from all and all again, from you and your torch,
great mother gold, spiked out of your noble brow.
Burn and kiss and pierce.

Stars hide in raucous pink, the dream of cities
in bad sleep. Not here. Zero at this height,
minus five—the price to be away—the clear
steep awful heart of nothing, perfect
in its peace. All tongues foreign, nothing
spoken here. The glacier, stratified like
generations, cracks across its heart.

Each breath's a hook
I drive between each bone.

Goodbye, you burning town,
you loom borne down beneath the burning thatch,
walls crumbling into pyres. You, goddess running
from high heaven's wreck, bright scissors
in your bony claw, black thread
like hair against the glow.

I know
the price of knowing,
of falling into wordlessness, apart.

O lady of my heart.

WIND RIVER RANGE, WYOMING

## Solvay Trona Mine, June 30, 1994

The cage drops fast, through zones of deposition,
hung on humming steel rope in squared-off dark.
As underfoot, through steel grate, a light
glows yellow 1600 feet below the ground.
As we fall toward the earth-remembered sea
and hear, in shouts, the customs of the mine.

The dust-man, with a dust moustache, has mined
gold, coal and trona—intrusions and deposits.
Clotted magma, crystallized rot, evaporite seas,
slow-processed wonders in the heavy dark,
each age pressed thin and carried underground,
laid like quilts in bedrooms without light.

The cage cries out and stops. The yellow stranger, light,
does not belong, nor we—tourists in the rumbling mine.
Our eyes are stung with glare and crystals finely ground,
salt and carbonate from shallow oceans, dried, deposited,
welded like brown glass, the content of earth's dark.
We board a red jeep diesel truck to sail the buried sea.

He drives, too fast. "Two miles," he shouts. We see
cables writhing overhead, roof-bolts blurred, lights
boring, tunneling the hot and powdery dark.
Eyes. He backs into a side-cut as the whole mine
roars. A tractor forks a steel knuckle by: "Deposit
for the welding shop," he says, "here, underground."

"The miner's law," shouts Moses in the underground.
"Take too much and the roof falls in." And ancient seas
rush back. We follow a tunnel through the brown deposit

into mayhem: a shuttle swerves and barges into light
to puke on the howling belt. I catch a fragment — mine —
and bow to these machines, assembled in their self-made dark.

Pulsing dust, the thing he calls *The Miner* chops raw darkness,
guided by red laser beams, two tall discs harrowing the ground,
it booms and spews its broken harvest back to the mine,
boring a double circle, ∞, carving a floor with chain. "Y'see
that cable? There. Step *on* it when you cross. *Never* shine a light
in a miner's eye." "How far," I yell, "does it run — the deposit?"

"Farther than you'd wanna go," he says. "This old deposit
might outlast us both — years down here." We breathe their dark
and shrink into a drift as a shuttle hammers by. He goes. My headlight
dims, then dies. I fumble with it, far from my home ground,
as they walk away and turn a corner, go. Then, I smell the sea:
salt and carbonate, fear and methane, ocean's mind.

My light is dead. I stumble through the mine
dismayed, imagining fish eyes in deposition,
shuffling on a dusty floor no longer seen,
under black-nerved cables, as the hot, impounded dark,
floods back to claim this pillared underground,
and long for sharp, sweet, windy, burnished light.

Every miner learns the lack of light,
how long bones yearn, more gravity than mind,
for mineral bliss — the estuary and the deepening ground,
the comfort of all clumsy form deposited,
all dread and hunger given to the dark.
Earth-locked, I smell the rank breath of the sea,

And run, and corner blind toward a voice and see
legged silhouettes, a lurching porcupine of light;
as at my back, in sweat along my spine, darkness
calls the black eventuality that's mine,
black puddle with a leather glove deposited,
all memory in the hard and holy ground,

Broken, belted, hoisted, fired, and ground
for soap, toothpowder, soda, glass, and wine. See
the jeep? See us crowd in tight? The air's deposit
stings our eyes, haunts us as we roll toward the light
and tongue dry lips, taste blood, the blush of mind
in mindless ages, moving through rich days and darks.

Braced against ourselves in stiff, dark
coveralls, we board the cage, fly through the ground.
But the miners say you never leave the mine.
Its ore spins in your blood; under sky you see
rock walls and feel earth's burden, cherish light
in passing, love as air; know death as a deposit.

All joy and pain deposited, and married to the dark.
O house thick-thatched against light's rain. Powers underground!
We rise from the old sea's mouth. A cloud floats free
   above the mine.

LITTLE AMERICA, WYOMING

Note: Six months after my visit, on February 3, 1995, nearly one square
mile of the Solvay Mine caved in. The shock registered Richter 5.3 and ac-
cording to the U.S. Bureau of Mines was "one of the largest mining-related
seismic events ever recorded." Fifty-three miners were on shift, and ten
were injured. Two were trapped for several days before they were found,
and one, Michael Anderson, died before reaching the surface. It was later
reported that for several years the support pillars had been decreased in
size, or "shaved," to increase production.

# The Hag

*from the Cheyenne and the Greek*

Waits, by the piled-stone well,
hungering. The fire around me
carries my body to the dark,

And they burn, white spume
torn off the sea, two long rips inside
my forearm's bulge: two seasons and two trees.

And back of the knee, the early
wound that gaped once, wet and rosy
so to kiss the wandering air.

A feast of scars:
Rope-burnt, the broad thumb's root,
hands world-bitten, horse and wolf and snake,
and mica in the crag that glimmered
through breath rising in the sun.

She looks; my right hand turns, a kicked stone
sutured at the knuckles where
blind steel slipped between,
saw light again.

Leave me my eyes, eater of ruined meat,
Old Bitch, I need them for the night,
black water that I see below.

Beside the heaped-up stones
she broods and mumbles in the gray arch
of her burning breast,

The old grape-bleeding song—
*O Dionysus, I did not know,*
*I did not know.*


The Cheyenne tell of a hag who inhabits the border of death and survives by eating the scars of those who pass. If the dying one is unmarked, then she devours both eyes. The lines to Dionysus were once, and may still be, sung by Greek women treading grapes.

# The Closing of the Sky

The Christmas pine,
set out forty days,
still holds its green,

needles still bound by fasciae
like slender hope, as if, despite,

something, dreams, the frozen root
buried in the mountain, miles north,

could rise and fly, to kiss
and resurrect the severed tree.

BOULDER, WYOMING

# In Gravity National Park

Now the sacred groves are cut
and burned to stave off
quiet and cold and dark,

the impulse rises, still
to hallow something
for such wonder and delight
as we have left,

something overlooked,
unvalued, obvious as fear:
simple, binding force as refuge
from the smoldering wreck.

Gravity's pristine, a field
unplowed. Takes all space
and none—a marvel, so

these rusty towers crowded,
just as any place, adorned
with signs, exhibits, diagrams
of falling bodies, moons and tides,
the way all things cohere.

Then, great gulps of space,
small hands in larger ones,
the jostling, shuffling lines,
openings designed for heads
and hands in chain-link fence

where we gaze down, shiver,
sigh, turn away

to buy small relics
(terra-cotta busts of Galileo,
spun-glass butterflies)
to drop and watch them break.

EMPIRE STATE BUILDING / ARCHES NATIONAL PARK

P A R T

# For the Listener

*The body dies, the body's beauty lives.*

—*Wallace Stevens, "Peter Quince at the Clavier"*

# The Mink

*for Ken, on New Year's Eve*

In winter, like a flame
blown sideways, blacker
than black water, loping,
curved above the current
in the ice's deadly glow.

Body like a riffle's image
lifted out and shaken
from the river's supple dream,
hungry round the boulders.
On a point of ice, he stops,
dips, grows, and dives,
black into the black.

One long breath, suspended,
two, and three, and hold—
the sleek, heart-pointed snout
rises to the far-bank ice. The mink
emerges, shudders, flexes, stops:
burnt cross barred with silver: trout,
struggling, whole, half-bitten-through,

And four, they're gone.
The river freezes, flows. Too cold
to stand, let alone to think,
I go, as night composes night,
half darkness and half sense,
blooms in the willows,
bleeds into the water,
as the first star swims up into view.

LOGAN RIVER, UTAH

# Old cars and trucks

Near the end of a washed-out road,
sandstone rises, warm as peaches at sunset
and there's an old mine,

toppled wheels and frames,
dead snakes of cable, rusty chain,
split ponderosa boards buffed silver,
spent Reos and Model A's that bore
this heaviness down and couldn't climb
the slickrock trail home—

were left for dead,
out beyond the light,
to weather, stripped
of useful parts.

On doors swung wide
at crazy angles to the light,
rust blooms, assured and slow
under factory blues and greens
no longer uniform: skies and meadows
daisied with rust. Not death
but hard intentions going
small and scattered, rosy oxide
stirred in red-gold sand,
easy enough to move with air,
to hold the floral print
of a mouse's foot.

CALICO BASIN, NEVADA

# Elegy *for Edward Abbey*

I'd like to say that coyotes passed the word along,
that leafless willows dreamed it up the roots of cottonwood
and sage along each muddy stream. I'd like to say the Colorado
told the Green, the Escalante, the San Juan, that grief
rose up each tributary to the melting snow.

Or that he sat out on some overlook, apart,
the sunset flaring up behind a blue-dark roll of storm,
composed a final question as the gust-front tugged his sleeve
and caught a bolt—the years of pain condensed, a flash.
That thunder punched the windows out

In Bluff and Blanding, every door kicked open
with the blast, walls suddenly uncertain, fences hung and buried,
every scrap discarded on the desert plucked and howling homeward
on that wind. That every rimrock shuddered, wept
red blocks of sandstone, pounding the tattoo.

I'd like to say the wished-for vultures carved
those long bones clean as limestone in the sight of sky.
If words are truth despite our eyes, then I'd say that. The father
of our grinning anger's gone; I never knew him better
than in song, the page turned in a thousand lights.

If empty beer cans all fill up with grace
then there's a heaven. The red sand drifts them full
beside the road, abolishes their names, buries them like books
with titles worn away by hands, a legacy mysterious
as strata, hidden and revealed: the holy land.

Pretty lies that please the heart are true
to that extent. The desert—no one's place—collects its patience,

love, indifference: we don't know. We know our loss, our
   desperation
when the burnjng space that hiked and pissed and laughed fills up
with air, when silence runs it through and through.

WEST OF ARCHES, UTAH

# The River

Maybe what I'll do:
walk down to the river,
walk down on the trail
where sand loves my feet
and wants to keep them.

Maybe I'll walk down, slow
as these red-and-black ants
when the long shadow covers us,
alone and cool on the trail,
looking around, half dreaming,
through cottonwoods with lamb's ear leaves,
seeing how tamarisk and Russian olive
chase coyote willow from the floodplain,
meandering among the thorns.

Maybe these thin lines of blood
incised by my direction
are tributaries to the whole notion
of going on: the necessary river
red and gold with earth, here
and gone through sandstone canyons
into the low sun as clouds return
full and flush with watered light,
bound for headwaters.

Maybe I'll get there soon,
drop my shoes and leave
a whorled print in slick silt
next to a raccoon track;
step down in and stand there looking
as muddy, cool mountain water
parts around my skin:

Maybe this is how it is.
Maybe this is how it is.

SAN JUAN RIVER, UTAH

# Looking up at you

*for Linda*

The lake's cool fingers
closed round my floating heart;
sly darkness wavered on the left,
around the point.
I swam away.

Swam along the drop and watched
trout rise like curving stars,
stroked the slick and naked limbs
of sunken trees, and felt the long December night
come freeze the surface of all play.

Nothing of the day
could call me back. Green boulders fell to black
beneath my flight, the open bay.

Water parts. Be swallowed,
like a final breath. Not lonely,
death, but soft support,
tempering the blaze. Easy,

slipping into cutthroat grace,
arms without a trace of selfishness,
broken-bottle gleaming round,
soft glassy green, for fools.

True, and true again, I thought.
Turn and swim. Breathe.
The boulders rise and glow,
as the point thrusts out, gold
shallows, pebbles, fingerlings.

I stop. Touch granite
with my foot and raise my face,
as you cry fear and welcome,
love, siren of the broken shore.

FRÉMONT LAKE, WYOMING

# Sacrament with pitcher pump

The water table's close.
The handle of the pump is cool inside my grip.
I feel the valve give way. Lift,
and it falls from the iron mouth
across my lips. Rusty tang, then
cold water from the aquifer beneath
hot sand, cottonwoods, dry grass.

Swallow and the ceremony moves,
as cells accept the gift,
into the circling blood
to bless a body's fire
with harmony: the touch
of hand to iron or voice to air.

At the wedding, water into wine.
And then the wilder change within
the husk of every drunken guest:
fruit-stained water into carnal broth,
natured in the whirling blood,
the flash of eye to eye, a grip,
the drum of dusty feet
as dancers form the ring,

familiar as our flesh.
Miracles, it seems,
are known things
out of place: a woman
floating in the sky,
voices without bodies,
wine in water jugs.

BOULDER, WYOMING

59

# Early

Light opens, wild blue flax.
We breathe ourselves aware.
The old three-legged cat descends
the attic stair, k-tump, k-tump,
a perfect heart.

The hollow boards ring low;
the inner walls absorb the beat
and give it back, immense,
contained in cornered logs
as if by bone, the flesh's heat
resounding, drumming all awake.

The stairs give into quiet rooms.
The cat is just a cat. Lost her left front leg
to a car's front wheel. She scratches
round her bowl and cries,

and still I hear that beat:
hollow stairs, the house's heart.
Whatever principle I choose
to draw the next breath by.

And soon the cat triangulates
onto the flanneled bed
where my good love and I both lie,
to push her thoughtless head,
bone hard and finely furred,
between our wandering hands.

BOULDER, WYOMING

# Full October

Moon turns the meadow
white, each frost-cured strand of grass
combed out by night. Apart,
two hundred miles northeast, a mile above
my wife, I feel the round beat of her heart.
Seven hundred miles west, the tide
surrounds the soft, cupped siltstone
up the coast from Pescadero.

My love's already lost in her, so
a sailor's ring slips
in the laying of the net.
Owls blink at my voice, here
pines and firs contain all sound, the meadow
opens like a body, clean and cold,
forgetting thunder and green days
for snow.

The first half of the night
I slept, dreamed of water,
hands upon my face, her hair,
and woke to this:
the glitter of scoured granite,
frost, the perfect, empty weight
of moonlight on the Great Divide.

ELKHEART PARK, WYOMING

# Fishing for brookies in the Boulder Ditch

It's prettier than it sounds:
October's dark, lucid green
runs pooled along the cobbled hill,
quarrels down short gravelly drops
through cottonwoods in gold.

Bending down, half-old
this morning, turning up the rows
I plucked worms rubbery with chill
in the broadfork's wake, caged them
in a cheese-dip can I found.

Later, leaving this home ground
I cross the cattleguard, follow a track
unbraiding into trails, like all good roads,
through sage, rattling lupine pods,
rabbitbrush, tall and bold,

blond as a stripper's hair
above the body's softer glow.
Under the ditch the meadows have been mowed,
the summer's grass compressed,
stacked in shaggy blocks.

Water never tires. The rocks
deflect but never stop that shining
work: erosion, deposition, willows, trout.
Harmonic, barbed as any hook,
forgiveness, plump and fair

beckons from the bare
blank shine, that flowing dark.

Along the west, lightning bolts thrust out
and blue clouds rise and thunder,
shadows walk.

The worm writhes
at the hook's quick going-through.
I cast to the broken run above the pool,
see a swift, green crescent moon,
feel the tug. Desire betrays

us, all good fish, plays
through the pole's quivering tip
and strums the line. I draw her from the cool
accustomed heavens to my hand.
My grip releases eggs, a tithe

to the moss. She
quivers, slick, hooked
at the hinge of her jaw, no fool,
to strike and swallow hard on pain,
or count the days.

Keep her wet. Raise
the shank and clip the barb away,
with steady hands and stainless fishing tool.
Relax your grip until she swims,
a spotted beauty, free.

BOULDER, WYOMING

# "Enter my dreams, love"

*after a line by Czeslaw Milosz*

In our slow-growing year,
with frost in every month,
I left the grass unmowed,

let the narrow forage build,
moon by moon, watched
seedheads form. Refuges
are few in this cold light,

our history, the close of sky
with low, blue cloud, a storm
that will not stay. Thin flakes
hold the air, hide mountains,
senseless, repetitious power.

As snowbacked heifers gather
to the fence, crop the tawn thatch
softening with fallen sky,

sleek and shaggy, rust and black
and cream beneath the white,
a cottontail comes under the wire,

under the low pine rail, stops
and settles, sees the inner yard
for what it is: grass, uncut and free,

small courage spared the whirling
knives. In other years, less hard,
I kept it neat, watched rabbits starve,

kept mine and winter's count.
In love or dream the world,
if we are lucky, is begun;

in snow or unmown grass,
a wish that one thing live
for one thing left undone.

BOULDER, WYOMING

# For the Listener

*after a poem by Wallace Stevens*

The winter mind regards
all moving things as curious: the falling angels
of the snow, the wild relief of avalanche,
black maples cracking with a shiver
on their own clear, frozen blood.

As branches slip their gathered snow,
spring back like lashes at the sky,
a dark bird falls (I later looked it up —
brown creeper), lies immobilized,
a blot against the snow's blue light.

I cup it, limp, still warm,
between my palms and hear
the wind rise in some other world.
This shadowed grove is still. As sunset
flowers on the ridge, my heart
and lungs make racket
in my body's ground.

The brown bird wakes
and watches me,

shivers, struggles, calms,
spreads her wings within my hands.
I set her free. Her claws dig in, she flashes up
and disappears. The sound
of wings is nothing
like the wind.

WHITE HORSE VILLAGE, UTAH